When Love Isn't Enough

LIFE AFTER DEALING WITH A NARCISSIST

Jessica D. Washington

IGNITED INK 717

Ignited Ink 717
Houston, TX

Cover design: Porsha Jackson, England Graphix
Page design: Ebony Rose, Ignited Ink 717
Photographer: MWhitley Media

Non-Fiction / Self-Help / Narcissistic Abuse

Jessica D. Washington is available for keynotes, panels, book talks, and workshops.
Visit JessicaDWashington.com to learn more and book Jessica.

Discounts for bulk purchases of 25 books or more are available. Visit JessicaDWashington.com to learn more and place an order.

ISBN, print: 978-1-7352286-7-9
ISBN, ebook: 978-1-7352286-8-6

Printed in the United States of America

Dedication

This book is dedicated to my sons, Jamyrion and Kaylon Washington-Lee

I never meant to bring you into this world to hurt you; I only wanted to love and cherish you.

I am truly sorry for any trauma that I have caused with my poor choices and decisions with bringing people in y'all lives to hurt you.

Love, Mommy

Acknowledgments

First and foremost, I would like to thank God for guiding me through this journey. I owe an enormous amount of gratitude and appreciation to those who assisted me through this journey and believed in me when my book was only a small idea. All of you spent countless amounts of time being my support, encouraging my growth, listening to my shit over and over for years and hours on end.

To George, Vanessa, Marquetta, Nadege, Kaisha, Lashaun, Ronald, Natalia, Tracy, Felipe G, Emonnie, Janella, Charlie, Desiree, Courtney, Victoria, Kimberly, Danny, Quartney, and the whole Atlanta F9 (Frontier Airlines) family, you guys have no idea how much I love and appreciate your support. This book would not have been possible without you.

To my dad, one of my biggest supporters, thank you for believing in me. You have supported my thoughts and ideas from day one. You pushed me to continue writing when I almost gave up, and you saw something in me that I couldn't see in myself. For that, thank you so much.

To my mama, thank you for showing me people can change and evolve into who they are destined to be. I know that we all faced many trials and tribulations, and we all have grown through our situations.

To my co-author Sad Reneé, I would like to take the time to show my gratitude for your assistance with writing my first book. You worked hard and spent many endless days and long nights working with me on my book. When I said I had doubts about my book, you encouraged me to keep going. You have rooted for me and pushed me well above measure.

You have been my go-to for everything, including this book. You are the rock that held this book together. Without your dedication, this would never have come together as well as it did. I owe it all to you. You were the puzzle pieces to this wonderful creation. I came to you with all the notes that I had been writing to myself for a long time now and helped me turn them into one of the greatest stories I've ever told. Thank you for all your hard work.

To my publisher, Ebony Rose of Ignited Ink 717, I would like to say thank you for believing in my vision from our very first encounter. You have maintained a professional demeanor; however, your authentic personality gained my trust. I hoped you would handle my masterpiece with care, and you did not disappoint. You have encouraged me from day one and helped me see the vision through manifestation and prayers. I shared my goals and dreams about my book with you before I shared it with people that's been in my life forever. I was IGNITED, inspired, and motivated to keep writing. Thank you for your patience and creativity. I am forever grateful.

Table of Contents

Chapter One

THE NARCISSIST

nar·cis·sist
/ˈnärsəsəst/

noun
a person who has an excessive interest in or admiration
of themselves.
narcissists who think the world revolves around them

Narcissist: Evil or misunderstood?

Narcissistic Personality Disorder is a mental condition in which the person may have an unquenchable thirst for admiration, attention, and a gargantuan ego. They do not possess empathy and lack the capacity to care for the needs of others and will put their needs and wants above all else. There are individuals who may be unaware of their dysfunction and are just displaying trigger responses to their own trauma. Then there's the person who is calculated, predatory, and genius in their craft. When does the former become the latter?

"You use up everything you've got trying to give everybody what they want." – Nina Simone

If you are ever on the receiving end of the narcissist's never-ending demands, you may find yourself asking, perhaps begging, for clarity on what they are seeking from you. But what narcissists want from their partners isn't a valid question because truth be told, they want whatever you must give them. It's not as simple as wanting your time, devotion, and trust. They want your life, to possess you.

As you give more of yourself, you will soon realize that you have nothing left. One day you'll look at your reflection, and you'll see yourself as a shell, empty eyes staring back at you, void of cognizance and full of resentment. You won't remember what you want or care about or what you sacrificed to be where you are.

Eventually, you will stare into the eyes of the narcissist and realize that you'll never be enough. This epiphany came to me after I had already lost myself, and it seemed like I would never reclaim who I was or wanted to be after divorcing the narcissist that I lovingly called my wife.

I found her in a crowded group of lesbians who shared an undeniable lust and attraction for each other as they embarked on their hunt for someone to fuel their hunger for love, attention, and affection. I didn't know it at the time, but the storm that tore apart my life would be floating around in this tiny yet vast space bigger than my ego, perhaps bigger than the world. I allowed myself to drift in this space of denial and unawareness, and she used that to her advantage.

You see, online dating gives you this anonymity to be whomever you want to be. In hindsight, I should have known that a person who would allow me in her life after what I would now describe as a few lifeless exchanges would have boundaries that she would eventually require for me and ignore for herself.

The night after our first meeting, we spent hours talking. In those moments, I felt intrigued by her military background, excited because she spoke of our future, and flattered as she said she had been watching me for a while. I was engulfed in feelings of amazement because she felt cultured and had a bit of sophistication to her. I believed her to be the ideal partner, one who understood responsibility, commitment, and honesty. If I am being completely honest, which I aim to be throughout this book, I ignored an endless parade of red flags, but my experience with narcissists did not begin with my marriage. It started at home.

Although I can attribute my abandonment issues to my mother, I cannot say that she had a place as a narcissist in my childhood. She and I grew closer as I grew older. While I still carry pain from her actions and negligence, I am proud of her growth in her journey of sobriety. Like any child holding resentment and any mother who is tired of apologizing, we often have disagreements that end in weeks of silence.

My mother must have her way. I am the daughter of a slick mouth hustler, and I find myself being guilt-tripped into doing things that I may not want to do. She told me who my ex-wife, Marjorie, was from the beginning, but I disregarded her opinion. Maybe out of rebellion, or maybe I looked at her own history with relationships and couldn't see pass her failures.

Along with having a slick tongue and an unapologetic personality, my mother is a self-proclaimed narcissist, and I could never tell if her declaration was out of defiance to me or simply because she realized her own toxicity. After telling my mother my plan to write a book about narcissism, she asked me to define the term narcissist, so I gave her a few examples. A few weeks later, she tells me that she is a narcissist, and she has always known that she had narcissistic traits but that she did not know the name for her disorder.

I felt relieved that she was taking accountability for her actions and that I was not crazy for the feelings that walked beside me for so many years. The realization that if only she had worked through her own trauma many years ago, our relationship could be different brought frustration and tears because having a better relationship in my adulthood wasn't enough. That abandoned child inside me yearned for her mother, and it pained her that she could never have that relationship. Anger and resentment reared its head because she was aware that she was not mentally well, but she didn't bother to get help.

My life could have turned out so differently, but instead of harboring ill feelings, I now feel hopeful that since she has put those words into sounds, maybe we can move forward. Perhaps I could talk to her without her defenses building 100 feet tall. Maybe, just maybe, we will be alright.

My great aunt and her husband are the heart of my trauma. It's what keeps my relationships from flourishing, emotional intelligence from expanding, and my mental health growth stunted. The abuse inflicted upon me was 20 years ago, yet I remember the gaslighting like it was yesterday. I can still feel my heartbreak as my aunt with whom I shared the same blood denied my truth and berated me with insults to twist my abuse at the hands of her husband.

"You're too black."

"No one touched you."

"You're a liar."

She said that I was too ugly, so her husband could not possibly want to touch me, but he did, and his sins stained my shadow to the point of ruin. Cleansing is impossible. For most of my life, I didn't dare to speak of this abomination. I now speak my truth. He raped me, and even though they are both deceased, I'm still a prisoner. I feel that I am still blacklisted within my own family, which forced me to find comfort and solace in the seediest places.

I had little-to-no guidance in my adolescence. I was stewing in all my anguish and was only a few disappointments away from going bad. The disparities between me and my peers were vast. They had stability and security. They seemed to have a foundation that encouraged their confidence and soothed their worries (as if they really had any worries). I prayed for a bit of saving grace, for someone to come along and believe me and believe in me.

My angel was my Aunt Earline, rest her soul. She became my heroine even in her imperfectness. She took me in and showed me beauty within myself. She nurtured me. She fed me. She gave me a safe space and became a pillar in my adulthood. We never want to go home as adults, but Aunt Earline was my home. And even though she eventually kicked me out of the nest for my own reckless behavior, she is still the most consistent mother figure in my life

Aunt Earline wasn't my only angel. Marla was my second foster mother, a diva clothed in holiness, sass, and class. She was well respected, and I admired that. She showed me a different side of myself. She helped me to find my femininity. She laced me with style and confidence. I coveted her strength. I don't think that until the moment that I walked through the threshold of Marla's home that I had ever encountered someone like her. She and her husband never argued in front of us. For the first time in my life, I ate at a dinner table, like a family. It was a scene from a movie; the mother and father had permanent marks of adoration while we teens and children engaged in conversation. We laughed. It felt unnatural. No one did this in real life. I lived in what I would describe Marla's home as a fairy tale for two years. If only I could have replicated that into my adulthood.

My adulthood heroine was Mrs. Shawn. Now, Mrs. Shawn's love was tough, loud, and unrelenting. She was my ex-manager turned godmother turned idol. She took me under her wing and tried to protect me from the predators within my life. One time she withheld my check because she did not want me to give it to the father of my children. Instead, she gave me just enough money out of her own pocket to pay all my bills. She was street smart and gave me the wisdom I desperately needed. She had this intelligence that, to this day, I cannot explain. She took me grocery shopping. She was the only person in the delivery room for my firstborn and to take me bra shopping. I walked into Lane Bryant, an 18-year-old wearing ill-fitting bras and walked out one step towards mastering womanhood.

Being thrust into motherhood at 20 was traumatic. The

father of my children is a master manipulator and ultimate narcissist. He was in jail during the birth of my firstborn, where he consistently love bombed me with false promises and lies. Each letter was a figment of his illusion of the kind of man he would never be and a life we would never live. His denial of his infidelity left me doubting what I knew and what I saw.

Everything was my fault, from my pregnancy to his failures. He blamed my lack of support for his incarceration. If I had not angered him, he would not have entertained other women. Accountability was unknown to him.

So, I must take accountability for my lack of knowledge. I would be 33 before I mastered womanhood. Motherhood is a journey, but I no longer allow my trauma to find its way into my children's subconsciousness. I can identify red flags. I know my worth. I am growing. I am healing.

Note to Reader

There are various types of narcissists. The most common types of narcissists are covert and overt.

Dr. Aaron Kandola describes covert narcissists (also known as vulnerable narcissists) as shy, withdrawn, or self-loathing. They tend to play on their victims' feelings of abandonment, fear, obligation, and guilt by exposing their own vulnerabilities, only these vulnerabilities never really exist.

It is only a ploy to create a faux safe space for you so that you can continue to trust them and confide in them. The feelings of obligation to share your truths because they did become overwhelming as you subconsciously enter a game of cat and mouse. You will crave that bond that you thought you had with the narcissist and overshare to try to duplicate that bond, but it will not come back. It can't come back.

When the victim has an unhealthy attachment to their abuser, this is known as *trauma bonding*. So, as trauma bonds are created, the victims are often left feeling responsible for the narcissist's emotions and will do anything to keep them happy.

While most people do not like to be criticized, covert narcissists are super sensitive to even the simplest form of criticism. They are envious and always compare themselves to other people, which leads them to be hypocritical. It is overwhelming dealing with their captious character. Everyone in your life is placed under a harsh microscope. Do you defend your friends and family to the death of your relationship? Or do you simply ignore them in hopes that their verbal vomit will be brief? Their anger or any strong show of emotion is never on display publicly. Covert narcissists are the most subtle because of the persona that they create. Helpful and nice to the public but emotionally and verbally abusive in private. They pride themselves on having humility and being humble when in reality, they find faults in others to boost their need to feel superior. This type of narcissist, in my opinion, is one of the most dangerous because their charm and faux niceness have the potential to convince even those you love that you are a person of deplorable character.

On the other hand, overt narcissists are more public with their toxicity. They are what I would call the poster child for narcissism. They are filled with aggression and animosity; they aren't shy or sly with their actions. They make no apologies for who they are; they will often demand remorse from their victims, not because they did anything in particular, but because it makes them feel powerful. They have huge egos and an unhealthy competitive spirit. They must be the center of attention at all times, and when they aren't, they will do whatever they can to have the spotlight they desire. They lack empathy, and experts say that they are incapable of love. They are usually aware that your friends and family hate them, but they do not care because they enjoy the thrill of being able to control others in that capacity. They will belittle their victims in public and dare onlookers to challenge them. They are dangerous as their rage is severely unpredictable. Their victims will pay for their impulses at a high cost.

There are many subtypes of Narcissistic Personality Disorder, and they all look different. The hybrid narcissist takes many forms, a chameleon, if you will. One minute they may be overt or covert, and the next minute they may be a cerebral narcissist, the narcissistic type that knows everything about everything. They will not pass up the opportunity to flex their accomplishments, education, and status and will expect praise and adoration. They thrive on being God-like, and your admiration is exactly what they need.

My ex-wife was an overt narcissist. She never tried to hide

her dysfunction and toxicity. Whether we were having lunch with my family on a visit to Houston or she was shouting for me to end my phone call, she was infamous for her obnoxious and cringe-worthy behavior. Marjorie had a way of being so sure of herself that she convinced herself that she could convince others that her behavior was acceptable. I can't count how many times I have had to apologize for her in-your-face attitude and her aggressive personality. She's had verbal altercations with family and friends and never bothered to apologize for her unacceptable and uncouth behavior. A part of me believed that she put on these outlandish performances because she knew that my loved ones would talk about her, and she loved the attention, good or bad.

Should you come across a narcissist, you should make plans to leave them or disengage as soon as possible. Things will not get better, and they will not change. Research as much as you can and then research more. You can never do enough. It's important to be educated on their traits and habits to adjust the expectations you have within your relationship.

Make an exit plan, journal, find a therapist, create boundaries, and gain a strong sense of self by journaling, establishing your own values and boundaries, setting goals, and accomplishing those goals. You will need a support system, which may be very hard to maintain, but it's not a suggestion. It's a requirement. The mental chaos can be draining, and you may find yourself giving in from exhaustion. Your life is worth fighting for. Your heart, peace, and emotional well-being are worth fighting for. You are worth fighting for. I hope you find love in your life after dealing with a narcissist.

Chapter Two

THE PERFECT MATCH

What kind of person is the narcissist attracted to? Why did my ex-wife choose me? I would like to believe it wasn't my low self-esteem that made me irresistible. I would like to believe it wasn't my weakness or stupidity that she saw that made me sexy. The truth is, how I viewed myself didn't matter. It only mattered how she felt and how I made her feel, how these traits supplied what her ego needed.

When we first met, I wasn't poor, but I was living the typical working-mom, middle-class life with just a few temporary debts and hardships, which she was aware of. My financial woes gave her the chance to swoop in and convince me she could be my hero. I believed that we could build something meaningful together, but I was ignorant to the fact that she had exaggerated her income, status, and abilities. Perhaps she could sense my deepest desires and hear what I did not say. She felt the pain of my inner child, the child that just wanted her mom to be a part of her life. The child that prayed for safety. The child that wanted to be loved and protected. And she used that to her advantage.

While I may never know why my overt narcissistic ex-wife chose me as her victim, there are so many qualities that someone may have that would qualify them as the perfect target to a narcissist. They may seek someone who is sympathetic, empathic, forgiving, kindhearted, and understanding. They look for softness and will make futile attempts to rescue their partner. Someone struggling with their self-worth will be easy to manipulate and bend to their will, or perhaps they will go for someone strong-willed, accomplished, talented, and well put together so when they tear them apart, they can admire their hard work and marvel at their masterpiece.

THE EMPATH AND THE NARCISSIST

Empaths are a narcissist's dream. Their ability to be attentive, understanding, and sensitive to the emotions of others lands them in the tight and turbulent grasp of the narcissist. To understand the amount of damage a narcissist can inflict upon an empath, we must first understand what an empath is. Empaths are highly attuned to the emotions of others around them. Not only are they sensitive, but they also experience the emotions of others as their own. Empaths are good at reading the intentions and thoughts of their peers, so the question arises: how can they not read the intentions of a narcissist? How can they not sense deceit and dysfunction?

Empaths are human, even with their abilities. The loving qualities that make them great friends, partners, and loved ones can also be their demise. Forever forgiving and compassionate, the empath provides the narcissist with an endless supply of support, attention, and love. As the well runs dry, the empath may take on the narcissist's low vibrations and toxic mentality. The empath's need to heal and help their partner grows stronger as it is accompanied by their own self-doubt and deprecation.

The empath isn't weak. On the contrary, they have uncompromising strength and resilience, which is why the narcissist will stick around. Unrelenting in their beliefs, they will persist in their quest to find redemption in their partner until they have no choice but to accept their defeat when the narcissist finally discards them.

THE CODEPENDENT

It is in the narcissist's best interest to get their partners hooked from the beginning. They start by being vulnerable, open, and sincere. They want to gather as much ammunition for the war to come. They will over-commit early in the relationship by painting a picture of this beautiful life that they assume that their partners want. Clinging to their partner's every word, the narcissist takes mental notes of their tone, body language, facial expressions, and it's not because they are interested in their partner as a person. They are interested in what they could weaponize.

My ex-wife let me talk endlessly. She studied my relationship with my sons and knew my soft spots. I became completely dependent on her to validate my worth, how I parented my children, and my presence as a friend. Everything was completely dependent on her approval. Her opinion mattered so much that my accomplishments felt like failures if she did not acknowledge or praise them.

She anchored herself in a position of power and authority, and I let her lead. I nailed myself on the cross so many times for her sins and took the blame when I did nothing wrong, putting my household in unsafe situations to ensure her happiness. I needed her to feel like a part of the family so we could operate as a family.

My happiness and safety were dependent on her as well. My day was a good day if she was content and chipper, and jokes were funny only if she found them humorous. I never wanted her to feel low, so I always made sure to elevate her in anything she did, but I never received the same courtesy. So, you see, this dance of codependency was never meant for me to lead. I was always supposed to stumble, trip on my own two feet, waiting to hit the ground because we were never in sync. Our rhythms never melted into a single movement, and we lacked grace. I tried to change pace and rhythm to match hers, and I got pretty damn close, but still, our dance was terrible. You can't force compatibility, chemistry, love, or change. It must happen. It must be meant to be.

Chapter Three

LOVE BOMBING

is an attempt to influence a person by demonstrations of
attention and affection.

I find it fascinating how a simple compliment or kind gesture can make us susceptible to those who sit on the lap of the puppeteer. Most of us learn the skill at an early age. We butter up our siblings so they may do our chores. We may be extra nice to our parents before asking them for new shoes or money.

Flattery can get you places and boy, did my mother, Erica do so. Her love bombs consist of telling me that she loves me and my kids. In her very dramatic and humorous manner, she says how life wouldn't be great without me and points out that I'm her only daughter. She usually follows up her ass-kissing by asking for a ride or a favor. If I say no, then an argument erupts. She makes promises to do things before asking for yet another favor.

You'd think that I would have noticed Marjorie's behavior from a mile away. I witnessed loved bombs detonate my whole life. I should have noticed her flattery accompanied with hidden intentions, but I ignored them. Maybe I enjoyed the intoxication that came with being the benefactor of her attention until it became something that I craved.

"I feel like you're my forever," Marjorie declared in a deep yet soft voice. We had only known each other for two weeks, but she had a dream that I was the one and could not see her life with anyone but me. She *prayed* for me. It was complete bullshit, but she was buttering me up for the deceit and mental trauma that she would bring my way, and I would let her.

My ex-wife would tell me that I'm the most beautiful person in the world. I'd awaken to good morning text messages coupled with inspirational quotes and flattering compliments. She could build me up skyscraper high. However, a few hours later, her words would become a wrecking ball; I'd be incompetent and worthless. There were days that I felt invincible. The strength that she would speak into me was exhilarating, so it only made me work harder for her approval when she was so mean and heartless. I needed her to love me and want me.

Marjorie and I only had sex six times in two years because she completely controlled intimacy. Affection was seldom, but it was frequent when it was clear that she wanted something or if it made her look like a loving partner in public. Nothing came easy or free with her; I had to earn everything. If I were the wife that she wanted, she'd reward me with sex, or if she was simply impassioned enough. Anytime I initiated sex, she would deny me and say that she didn't feel like it for whatever reason. I always respected her space, but it only left me wanting more.

The last time that we were intimate was cheap but igniting

car sex. After 45 days of no contact, she texted me and said that she needed me to sign the divorce papers and really needed to talk to me. She showed up unannounced, and the first few seconds after I planted myself in the passenger seat were filled with silence. She stared deeply into my eyes as she complimented me, and my stomach filled with butterflies. It almost felt like when we first met, when her manipulation tasted sweet, and her presence was an honor.

We talked about our marriage and smiled at the good times, such as how we started our family and our trips to Vegas, Miami, and New York. We reminisced on how we met and blushed at how much we were in love. We talked about my youngest son – Kaylon's football season and our current interests and hobbies. She missed our family, and I admitted that I missed her too and was still in Atlanta for her. She admitted that she was not ready to sign the divorce papers, and when she filed, she was angry and confused. I really wasn't ready to divorce either and considered therapy.

We let our eyes linger, and she admitted that she missed my touch and asked if I wanted to have sex. My words became stuck in my throat, so I nodded yes. Our lusty breaths filled her truck, creating fog and longing. Somewhere between the kissing and friction, I dropped my defenses along with my clothes. The backseat became the bed that we once shared. Her fingers played notes that soothed my broken heart, and warmth overcompensated for the cold shoulders. Our love fest erupted into more chaos that would come. I left out of her truck void of dignity, and the divorce papers unsigned.

Marjorie canceled the divorce after our cheap encounter, but drama immediately overshadowed our lusty glow. It all started with a video she posted on social media about her accusing me of being an abuser and traumatizing her and her daughter, Sage. She contacted me and admitted that she had posted a video and that she didn't mean to hurt me. She blamed her accusations on the fact that she saw a coworker of mine who refused to speak to her and posted the video in defense.

I knew that this was really a ploy to get me to talk to her and get access to me, so when she confessed that she missed me and wanted to talk, I denied her request by telling her that I had to end the call. I was at home and didn't want to talk to her in front of my children for fear that they would be severely disappointed in me.

We began to communicate constantly, and I found myself caught in her trap again. Marjorie was a proud woman, and here she was, being vulnerable with me as she stated that she felt embarrassed by strangers knowing her business. She expressed her pain and regret filing papers and pushing me away.

Prior to this exchange, she posted a video bashing me as a partner and parent. After her slam video went viral, she made another video saying that she loved her wife and her family and told her followers to never give up because we all make mistakes. She disguised her fluff and love bombing as wisdom. Sage became a pawn as she used my love for her to continue to lure me by telling me that she wanted to speak with me and she missed me.

Eventually, the cat was out of the bag. The kids knew that we were in contact and were considering making the relationship work. I'm not sure how Sage felt about it, but my boys were strongly against reuniting our family. They let me know of their disdain for their former stepmother and never passed up a chance to insult her. I think they were trying to make me feel better, but I always wondered what they really thought of me.

Admitting that I let someone sweet talk me into submission is humiliating, but it is deeper than that. She controlled my every move. There was no way that I could have out-maneuvered her because she was always ten steps ahead. She knew my insecurities and what I desired most from life, for myself and for my family. I realized that it wasn't as simple as sweet talk, and the person I loved never saw me in the way I saw her. She was a predator, and predators are incapable of love.

Note to the reader:

Random acts of kindness are always treasured in a relationship, whether romantically or platonically, but when dealing with a narcissist, it seems unfair that affection and love should be so costly. At the beginning of my relationship with my ex-wife, she wooed me relentlessly. She spoke words that a girl could only dream of, and it shook my world. She loved me so hard that I felt required to love her harder. I was blinded by the grenades that she was throwing at me.

Narcissists love bomb because they know what their victims crave -- love, affection, adoration -- and it's their primary form of control. Love bombing isn't consistent. It can't be. It must be capricious so they can use it as a pawn. They will create a love drought just to pour more into you once they feel like you are slipping away. They want you to be in remembrance of the good times during the dark times, but this is just an illusion that the narcissist has created to keep you in their grasp.

Please know that if it seems too good to be true, it usually is. Life is not a romance film. Few are lucky to experience love at first sight. Lesbians are notorious for moving very fast in relationships. Our love ignites so intensely and passionately that it often burns out just as fast, so it can be hard to see through the smoky haze of love bombing. Love shouldn't be rushed, so stand firm in your boundaries and talk to your partner if you find yourself being coerced into a commitment that you are not ready to make.

The feelings of desperation, loneliness, and eagerness to have a partner should not be a deciding factor to whom you give your time. Narcissists prey on people with these feelings as it's easier to get them to comply with their rules. Here are a few ways to deal with Love Bombing:

- Set clear boundaries and stand firm.

- Do not allow yourself to be rushed into a relationship, i.e., cohabitating, marriage,

- Respectfully and firmly reject gifts, trips, and faux acts of kindness

- You have flaws, and you are not perfect. Remember that when narcissists are passing out endless compliments.

- Create a healthy distance between you and the love bomber. They should not have 100% of your time to the point where you neglect your other relationships.

- Have a strong support system.

You will find love again, but settling is not an option. Focus on yourself, your goals, and the relationships with those who genuinely care for you. It will be hard to trust again after dealing with a love bomber but find a therapist to cope with your triggers and mistrust. May you find love in life after dealing with a narcissist.

Chapter Four

MANIPULATION

ma·nip·u·late
/məˈnipyəˌlāt/

verb
control or influence (a person or situation) cleverly,
unfairly, or unscrupulously.

My earliest experience with manipulation would be my great aunt and her husband. She often used manipulation tactics such as isolation and threats to silence the horrors they bestowed upon us. My aunt and uncle created this empty, lonely, hostile world for my cousins and me. They would lock us in the room and even went as far as to keep us away from other family members. To give context to their extreme isolation, I lived with my aunt and uncle since I was three days old, and the first family function that I attended was at the age of 9.

We were threatened with more beatings for just existing. My uncle, who would describe the sexual abuse as "playing," would ask me to bathe in hot water whenever we were done playing. To this day, I still do not understand why. His threats were horrifying. He would kill me if I ever uttered a word about his playtime.

I was unaware that something as simple as food was being used as leverage to force us to comply and keep us obedient and subservient. They would force us to drink Slim-Fast, and sometimes we just would not drink at all. We were banished from being inside the house for hours and were only allotted a pitcher of water between six kids, nothing more. We ate tuna out of the can with a slice of bread on the kitchen floor. While not even six feet away, my aunt and uncle would eat gumbo, chicken, shrimp, and fish, food that felt like a luxury. To gain our gratitude, they would say that our family did not care about us because we were children they threw away. Our parents were gone, and we had to live with that sin.

My mother, the grandmaster manipulator, has managed to cheat me out of time and money by leveraging her ability to be a grandmother and mother. A phone call is usually met with skepticism. I am a complete failure at her game of quid pro quo. A cigarette raises her availability to babysit or spend time with her grandsons. It's a risky game, one that leaves me feeling alone and 19 again.

The highest stake was one that I couldn't afford -- pay for her hair or buy her drugs. I found myself falling prey to her desires as she used her addiction as an excuse to guilt me and make me her emotional slave. Afraid that she would fall into the unknown, I often gave in and gathered whatever chips and pride I had left.

The line between control and influence is a fine one. As a society, we must be willing to admit that we are, in fact, subconsciously controlled or manipulated by the media. Artists we hold in high regard influence us to buy products and aspire to possess material items we can never afford. Executives sit in rooms and create ads to convince us that we want, well, need a product. They utilize certain colors to guide us into obedience, such as yellow, to bring about feelings of joy and acceptance. Are our thoughts, feelings, and desires our own, or are we doing exactly what society wants us to do?

In my case, I was completely unaware that my free will was held hostage by family members and my ex-wife. In retrospect, I was manipulated from the moment that Marjorie and I met. I declined her invite for company as I told her that I had no desire to go out. She explained that she would like to be better acquainted and spend time with me in person. It had been years since anyone had captured her interest enough for her to approach them. After other statements that inflated her fragile ego, she said that she had settled for everyone she had dated in the past year and a half, and she was only interested in what she wanted at the moment. The feelings of flattery drowned out all the warnings that the red flags were screaming at me. I felt important. Seen. That moment felt very authentic. She wanted me- I was *wanted,* and to be honest, that's all I ever really craved from not only my partner but from my family.

My ex-wife accomplished what she set out to do. She wanted me to feel honored, like it was a privilege to have her interest. She and various partners of my past had that in common. An expert at multitasking, they wore many faces. They were completely obsessed with their own impulses and desires, turning every situation into puppetry. They pulled the strings, and I performed to satisfy their every whim.

My ex-boyfriend, T, used his fist to intimidate me. He alienated me from my friends and family, and my sister, who is one of the closest people to me, became a stranger. I recall an instance where I crossed paths with my sister, and we greeted each other with blank stares and silence, her out of resentment and hurt, and me, out of shame and obedience.

His favorite control tactics were to use his age and wisdom to convince me that he knew best. He wanted the best for me, so I needed to be grateful and comply. T had a knack for speaking with self-importance. He was so self-assured that he never apologized when he would strike me. He would shut down and leave me licking my wounds alone.

While my ex-wife and I were certainly toxic, we only had one violent experience. I wanted to do something nice, so I purchased a gaming system for her. My thanks were vehemently praised by her saying that she hated my gift and insisted that I return it because she wanted to purchase it for herself. Honoring her wishes, I began to gather the gaming system. The sight of me holding something that

I purchased with my own money angered her so deeply that she shoved me.

Instinctively, I put my hand on her shoulders to keep her away. Her version would go on to say that I choked her. I believe that she knows that I was not physically abusive to her, but her persistent accusations of my phantom abusiveness were just a way for her to keep me in her control. If she could convince me that I was abusive, she would forever have a trump card to play against me. I am proud that I did not cower under her words, shoves, and illusions. I would have fought back if I needed to, but I am relieved it never got to that point

Looking at both of those relationships, they closely mirrored each other. Marjorie and T both caused a rift between me and anyone who would dare speak out against our relationship. Anyone who challenged their views or who dared to tell me the truth. I'd often bring the comparison to my ex-wife, and she hated the comparison, possibly because she knew if I left T, I could leave her too.

They both were only small in stature, which I believed contributed to their need to feel important and be in control. Only a truly damaged person must tear someone down to build themselves up to make up for their shortcomings. I cannot say that I have forgiven them completely, but I truly pity them because I don't think they have ever felt true love or are capable of giving it, and that is a sad, lonely life.

****

Those three years that I spent with Marjorie had to be my lowest. I was the embodiment of the walking dead. My heart and mind were disconnected. My spiritual self was deteriorating. Stress was my best friend. I found myself apologizing to Marjorie for being a disappointment, sensitive, and not being fun or humorous. I presented my true authentic self, and I kept apologizing for that, and every time I apologized, I destroyed pieces of myself to allow her to create who she wanted me to be. As much as I wanted to hate her and blame her for everything that went wrong at times, I hated myself more. So not only was I full of remorse, but I was also full of "if only." If only I weren't so naive. If only I didn't ignore the red flags and allow my desire to love and be loved to cloud my judgment. If only I were stronger. If only my childhood hadn't been a cesspool of trauma.

I was floating into the darkest place I had ever been since being a mother because I felt like I could not do anything correctly. Not only was I failing at being a wife, but now my children had front-row seats to the show that broadcasted my failures, insecurities, and shortcomings. I saw hatred, resentment, and disgust in their eyes whenever I managed to meet their gaze. I lost their respect, and at times, I felt that I didn't have the right to discipline them, teach them right from wrong. How could I when I was only a mother in the flesh? I was nothing.

I wish that I could forget that night. I wish that it never happened. I feel red with shame every time that I think about it. I could feel and hear the static in my head. My hands shook endlessly, and my heartbeat matched the pounding of drums, intense and hard. The faint but deafening sound of my ex-wife screaming at the top of her lungs, accusing me of being an abuser, among other things that hurt too much to write. The combination of everything that I have ever encountered triggered something dark in me, and I attempted to leave my kids motherless, my mother daughterless, and my siblings without a big sister. I regret that day, and hopefully, I will never do it again.

The Proposal

Our marriage was inauspicious by the engagement alone. After a month of dating, Marjorie proposed the idea of us living together. She wanted me and my boys to move to her small town in a much smaller community. I respectfully declined as I did not want to uproot my kids again after the move to Atlanta from Houston. A part of me knew that this relationship would be my demise, so I began my failed attempt at sabotaging the relationship. I tried to be as unbearable as I could be. My attitude was constantly changing. I'd start arguments in hopes that she'd break up with me or at least create distance. My attempts were futile. I realized that there was nothing that I could do to make her leave me at this point in her life because she received a letter in the mail informing her that her income would decline. She needed me now more than ever, and although I did not know it at the time, she needed me more than I needed her.

Three weeks later, Marjorie would propose to me during our Miami trip. Somewhere between the arguments and gaslighting, she managed to propose on the beach, which included a speech with a string of cliches such as "I loved you from the moment that I met you. I knew you were the one. I dreamt of you being my forever." It was nothing that I hadn't heard in the romance films. It wasn't unique or poetic, but still, I accepted her proposal.

At this point, I am sure that I seem insane. How dare I go through the trouble of trying to sabotage our relationship only to accept her proposal? She was a monster after all, wasn't she? The brutally honest answer is. I believed she could provide me with a life that would upgrade my current one. She is a veteran, so I imagined myself and my boys benefiting from her resources, and if we both pooled them together, then things may be alright. It was worth the troubling behavior that I was seeing from her. Would I rather be distressed in a two-bedroom apartment or my dream home?

AFTER THE PROPOSAL

Marjorie wormed her way into a permanent spot in my life. Once I accepted her proposal, I knew that I had officially lost control of my life and the relationship. She consistently downplayed my talents and accused my most innocent acts of duplicity. I was late picking up my son's medication, and the pharmacy contacted her to let her know the medication was ready. She accused me of being selfish for inconveniencing her life, which is ironic considering that I was scolded not even two days later for not picking up her child's meds after offering to get them.

Everything was a one-way street with my ex-wife. I first realized how sick she was when she accused me of wanting my stepdaughter to die. She brought my stepdaughter to my house sick, and I began to get ready to get her some medication from the drugstore when Marjorie declined my offer and said that she would bring the medication that Sage needed back home to me. She never brought the medication and, of course, accused me of being a horrible person, wife, and mom because I did not get the medicine that I offered to get in the first place.

I mentioned to Marjorie that I desired a new car as I had outgrown my Charger, so she went out and purchased a car for me. I thought that she was being thoughtful and caring, but I soon learned that it was all to control how I spent my time, where I went, and who I was with. When I agreed to a legal separation, she took the vehicle she purchased for me back, knowing that I needed it for work. She said that I would ruin her credit by not paying the monthly car note. My first act of defiance and independence was when I purchased my own vehicle after she took back the vehicle she purchased for me. She would later admit that she took the car back because she needed to teach me a lesson. She didn't know that I had money in my savings account, and that's how I was able to get a car two days later. She was infuriated and called me, spewing the worst insults that she could muster, and stated that she needed me to be able to call her to take me to work and errands. She realized that she could not use the car as leverage to control me. I am unsure if she respected me for how I was able to take care of myself, but that situation showed me that when I stared survival in the face in the midst of war, I would win every time.

I am not perfect. I have done my share of despicable acts, and I take accountability for all of my misdeeds. I cheated and manipulated an ex-partner into giving me money to buy a new car. I leveraged love to get what I needed or wanted out of my romantic relationships. I talked an ex-partner into moving in with me out of convenience for my life, disregarding what she would be giving up. During my marriage, I often entertained the idea that Marjorie was my karma for the things that I did to my ex-lovers, and I deserved every bit of her abuse. If my marriage was restitution for my crimes, well, I think that I certainly served my time.

Note to reader

Manipulation can range from joining a Multi Leveling Marketing company to emotional abuse. Susan Forward (author of Emotional Blackmail) describes fear, obligation, and guilt (FOG) as the three feelings that emotional blackmailers use to ensure their success of emotional trauma upon their victims. Emotional blackmailers such as narcissists will play upon your greatest fears and use them against you to get what they want, and obligation and guilt just creates a nasty, vicious cycle.

I want you, the reader, to understand that you have a choice: it is perfectly ok to say no. I felt obligated to do so many things that I really didn't want to do, and when I did attempt to stand my ground, I felt so guilty. The result? I would eventually give in to their desires even though I knew it was wrong to do so. So again, another cycle of FOG.

ESTABLISH CLEAR BOUNDARIES

WITH YOUR PARTNER.

Love shouldn't come with demands. Doing anything out of FOG is dehumanizing and will strip you of your dignity.

You are entitled to make your own decisions, mistakes, and have feelings. May you find your voice in life after dealing with a narcissist.

Chapter Five

GASLIGHTING

Gaslighting is a colloquialism that is defined as making someone question their reality. The term is also used informally to describe someone (a "gaslighter") who persistently puts forth a false narrative which leads another person (or a group of people) to doubt their own perceptions to the extent that they become disorientated and distressed. This dynamic is generally only possible when the audience is vulnerable such as in unequal power relationships or when the audience is fearful of the losses associated with challenging the false narrative. Gaslighting is not necessarily malicious or intentional, although in some cases, it is.

I always found myself walking at night. I never knew where I was headed or where I was coming from, but I always kept walking. I was usually alone, but the sound of the city, which played in an endless loop, became my companion. Street signs led me to nowhere familiar. I kept my pace because it felt good to be outside in the crisp air. This seemed to be the only time that I knew peace these days. I came to a fork and had to decide on which road to take. What I soon realized is that it did not matter which road I took. It always led me to hooded figures.

Rain poured from the sky, but my hands were dry. Though the wind was crisp, there was ice on the ground. I ran and skidded into a building, but I did not get hurt. I bounced back, and instead of falling, I hung in midair. I stayed there for what seemed like an eternity. Numb but in pain. I searched the darkness and found a glimpse of myself in the mirror. I wasn't floating. I was standing still, but when I looked at myself, I was indeed floating on my back with my face towards the relentless rain. I could not make sense of my reality.

That dream was recurring throughout my marriage. I felt so lost and incredibly confused. My dream reflected the reality I resided in. I was drowning without swimming. I second-guessed myself, my character, my desires, and my heart. Did she really slam my son to the ground? Was my will to paint her out to be the bad guy strong enough for me to create such a disturbing event inside of my head? Marjorie was intently adamant that she never laid a finger on him. Then, she made me question my sanity by throwing my latest mental breakdown, which landed me in the hospital, into my face—deflecting the attention from her actions and rerouting the argument to be about me and poor actions that never existed.

I want to clarify that being gaslit changes your perception of things over time. Little events created even bigger messes that I struggled to clean up. I was on my way to the mall and offered to take my stepdaughter and Marjorie to accompany me. She declined, but she started an argument as I was out the door because I should have asked her to go. Imagine my frustration as I tried to stand my ground. Needless to say, I never took that trip to the mall. Here's how things escalated:

I included her in all of my plans for my birthday, but somehow, she still found a way to make a day that was supposed to be dedicated to me about her because she didn't feel included enough. How selfish of me.

She asked me for a chocolate cake for her birthday, and when I presented her with one, she became angry because she suddenly did not like chocolate cake.

I went to every doctor's appointment that she ever had at the VA, but to this day, she will swear on every Bible available that I never did.

Our household became in disarray, so we tried to create order by assigning ourselves chores that we alternated. She insisted that I should clean up every day and called me trifling and accused me of not wanting to clean up. Now, this is when things really started to get skewed as I believed that maybe I was wrong and misunderstood our agreement.

My sons were not used to sharing me, and I wanted to give them individual attention. I explained to her that I would take my sons on individual dates. The first date belonged to my firstborn and the second date belonged to my youngest. In what I believe to be a fit of fury, she called me a bad mom because I didn't take them on a date together, and I did not know which son I said that I would take first. I now realize that she weaponized my childhood trauma with my own mother by convincing me that I was her when she was at her worst. One of my greatest fears was that I would fail my children. That I would not be able to provide for them as I desired, and she never let me forget those fears.

Along with weaponizing my childhood trauma to gaslight me, she also used my desire to create a solid bond with Sage. My efforts were often met with jealousy and resentment. She asked me to get the kids dressed on the first day of school while she rested in bed. She was the daughter I never had. I found joy in combing her hair and decorating her plaits with colorful bows that matched her dress. It was a pleasant change from the hours spent at the barbershop with my sons. Instead of acknowledging her daughter, she got upset and accused me of taking a very important moment away from her.

I didn't realize that she would set me up to always feel unworthy of her daughter. She asked me to make a poster for Sage, and when I did, she said that I tried to take over her parental duties. It truly felt like a punishment, but the more she accused me of cheating her out of moments with her daughter and failing with my own kids, the more I felt the need to prove to her and myself that I could be who she needed me to be: a dutiful wife, an attentive mother and life partner.

My firstborn has always been expressive. He continues to evolve and develop at a rate that I sometimes struggle to keep up with. There was a short time when he shared that he felt like he was transgender. While I was not entirely against his feelings of his identity, I thought it would be best to wait, see how he would develop, and set boundaries, but it felt like she was forcing the idea of being transgender on him more than he was ready to accept or deal with, but I knew my son.

I knew that he would have so many ideas and interests and did not want to make a permanent decision while he was still sorting through his own feelings. This would become another tipping point as her approval became disapproval as swiftly as his identity of being transgender. Not only was her ability to gaslight and twist every situation affecting me, I wonder if it played a role in him living his true self.

Not long after he declared his identity, he discovered that he was homosexual, and currently, he has now decided that he is a heterosexual cis-gendered teen. My love for him never wavered while he was discovering who he was or what he chose to identify as, but I continuously worry if he is walking in his truth. I know that I am not over the mental trauma from being with my ex-wife, and the thought of the long-term effects of my marriage on my children continues to haunt me.

I am not proud of many things that happened within our marriage, but I always thought my children would have the least damage since they were so young. I tried my best to hide the stress of my troubled marriage when the unforgivable and unthinkable happened.

My black sons were being accused of heinous crimes and labeled degenerates at home before society had the chance to. I always thought that the danger was outside. My home was safe. A haven where they could be themselves, live joyously in their blackness. It was a shelter from the other things they could face.

My stepdaughter accused my sons of touching her inappropriately, but she never told me personally because, as it was her right, Marjorie was her spokesperson. The accusations were not simultaneous but were a year apart. My oldest was accused first and, later, my youngest son. This messy and chaotic situation seemed very forced and instigated by other parties.

I have a few theories as to why my sons were the proxies. Before the situation happened, my stepdaughter's father was trying to take her away from my ex-wife. I was never privy to the details as to why he felt Sage was better off with him. Still, it always bothered me how she was so secretive about it. I was confused about why my ex-wife kept switching sides during this situation. One moment my son was being criticized so harshly by Marjorie that I had to question if she ever loved him. The next moment she would admit that she believed that my sons never touched Sage as she professed her love for me and our family. One moment she denied calling the cops and cps, and the next, she would say that she did not remember making the calls and that the situation was now out of her control. Later, she would say that she would have never made those calls if she had a choice. Bitterness, hate, and paranoia became my life because I just couldn't understand how or why this was happening.

It felt like my kids were taking the fall and my ex-wife was protecting someone else. While I still love my stepdaughter ferociously, I had no choice but to stand by my sons and believe them because I knew with every fiber of my being, this would be something that they would not be capable of. My sons never showed any sexual interest or curiosity towards her or other children, while my stepdaughter was unusually sexual, and her behaviors concerned me.

I would bring her behavior to Marjorie's attention, and it felt like she brushed them off every time I wanted to talk about it. While I am certain that my sons never touched her, it was clear that something was going on with her. My heart breaks for Sage. I feel that I should have been more persistent with my questioning, but I didn't want to continue to overstep my boundaries with her. For the sake of my sons, I had to deny her request to speak to her stepbrothers. I know that she must be confused, and I am sure she misses them. They were the Terrible 3. Always in mischief and covering for each other, but what was I supposed to do? Did I do the right thing? What could I have done differently? Did I fail my children? Did I fail my stepdaughter?

Even after all that happened, I still wanted to have a family. I wanted to try to mend our heartbreaks and trauma. I NEEDED to keep my marriage together. I sent my ex-wife a message saying that I wanted to be better than what we were, and the next day, I received this email:

Jessica,

Know that I have and will always love you. But I need you to understand why you are receiving this email. Within the last two weeks, your attitude, frustration, and defensiveness have led you to have to apologize for getting loud, aggressive, or rude during our conversations. As well, while at Sage's therapy this week, I came to realize that maybe we won't work because being together, in addition to what she claims happened to her last year coupled with your actions in the previous week and a half (which Sage overheard) may possibly be or become a trigger for her. Lastly, based on what you said last night, it's apparent that you desire more and different. I can't possibly give you that in the present or near future. Especially since you're on social media advertising that you're single and all....but I digress.

You will find attached the documents you need to have signed to add them to the filing if you're still willing. If not, please let me know at your earliest convenience.

That being said, I hope that your move back to Texas is a very blessed and prosperous one. I hope that you find what it is that you so desire since that is not me.

Marjorie.

I know that I should have ended the marriage after the first accusation, but it wasn't until the second accusation that I realized that we would never be a family again. In all honesty, I did not cut my ex-wife off right away. I was still in contact with her until the divorce was finalized. The day after, I blocked her and ignored every attempt she sent my way, even in my weakest and loneliest moments. I had to think of my boys. I had to think of my peace. I had to THINK and not get lost in my feelings.

Note to reader:

Gaslighting is meant to alter your memories, perception, and reality. A narcissist will discredit your truth, minimize your feelings, and monopolize your life. Gaslighting has many faces and can be quite subtle at times. It ranges from small lies to turning you against yourself.

Red flags to look out for:

- Narcissists will tell shameless lies. When presented with facts and truths, they will still lie or, even worse, find a way to make you believe their lies.

- They are all talk and no action. Rarely will they ever do what they say or follow up on it.

- They will defame your character to turn others against you.

- Their accusations and rhetoric cause you to constantly apologize for everything.

- Your self-worth is based on their opinions.

- You begin to look to them as your source of reality and make decisions for you.

Gaslighting is emotional abuse and mental warfare. Please do not let someone's sickness become your reality. It can be very hard to see through the fog. Find a way to anchor yourself, something that reminds you of the present. If you can, find a therapist, and if that is not possible, find a way to confide in a friend, someone who knows your character, will remind you of who you are, and isn't fooled by the narcissist.

While a monster to you, they can present themselves as the perfect mate, which means they may fool the people closest to you. It would be ideal for you to leave the relationship as soon as possible, but realistically most victims tend to stay past their expiration date, and some never leave due to embarrassment and ego.

I felt like such a failure walking away from my marriage, but I learned that I am not a failure for walking away. I was only a failure if I chose to be cowardly, chose the easy way out, and if I never tried to rebuild my life after dealing with a narcissist.

Chapter Six

SHIFT BLAMING
(Projection)
pro·jec·tion | \ prə-ˈjek-shən

Noun

the attribution of one's own ideas, feelings, or attitudes
to other people or to objects.

Imagine the only sense that you have is your hearing. You know you're not alone, but you can only hear one voice. That voice that sticks out is full of conviction, resentment, menace, and trickery. You're repeatedly told the same things. Everything that you do is wrong. Everything is your fault. You have single-handedly wreaked havoc on this person's life. You're ugly. You're worthless. You're useless. Your trauma is being thrown in your face. Everything is starting to make sense now. You're the cause of your mother's addiction. You deserved every violation. No one cares about you. You're talentless. You're an imbecile. You're unworthy. Congratulations, you now have all your senses. You open your eyes, and what do you see? What do you feel? Do you know who you are?

Narcissists are masters at deflection. Accountability is unknown to them. The idea that they are imperfect with faults is completely foreign and threatens the impregnable delusions that they have of themselves. One has to wonder how much it will take to convince yourself that the world is out to get you.

I sometimes wish that I could possess so much blindness. Maybe, I wouldn't have to stay awake at night and think of my mistakes and all the people I hurt. Maybe I wouldn't shrink under the shadows of my failures. Many opportunities stared me in the face, and I bypassed them all to serve my own agenda. I am still paying for my carelessness to this day. If I could convince myself that it wasn't me but everyone around me, what kind of person would I be?

I truly believed that I was who and what my ex-wife said. After so many attempts to be more than who she insisted that I was, I relinquished any power that I had. My mind was hers. We weren't connecting because I spent too much time on the phone. Most of my loved ones were hundreds of miles away in Texas, so having that open line of communication was important to me. She refused to give me quality time because she felt that I was giving too much of my attention away that belonged to her.

Wary of the arguments and craving intimacy, I stopped taking calls inside the house. We never communicated or bonded, and the distance between us grew wider. I had my loneliness and resentment to keep me company.

I was humiliated and ashamed to tell my friends and family what my life was like in its entirety. I would give them a peek, a small view of her ways, but they knew. My friends and family were against the relationship from the very beginning, and as blunt as they all could be, I am sure they held back much of their opinions to keep the peace and not push me away. At times it felt like they were walking on eggshells just as much as I was. It felt very unfair that they had to alter themselves because of the person that I was married to. There was no privacy; their deepest and darkest moments were on display as she would lurk and listen in only to weaponize their experiences and traumas as well. I felt sick knowing that I could not be present 100% for them in those moments.

****

It is important to know that gaslighting is very similar to blame shifting with very few differences. Both set out to do the same thing, contort their victims' reality through their never-ending need for power as their victims relinquish their free will. Their ability to admit their wrongdoings while absolving themselves of any responsibility is quite magnificent.

It was a form of art, the way that she painted me out to be a villain in every story. Each retort was my emotional and mental health being spread across the canvas. Messy and chaotic, colors are thrown violently, splattering against the wall. My triggers are momentum to her verbal abuse, a tribute to her. I feel she's memorialized, a dark, shameful part of my history. I pray that it won't take decades for them to be destroyed. I pray that there won't be an internal outcry within myself to hold on to them and her.

I pleaded with my ex-wife to go to therapy with me. We simply were not performing at our peak, and I had to try something. While I am not a stranger to therapy, I was not consistent with my appointments, and I thought this would be a great way to get back in the flow of things and help my marriage. My insurance did not include therapy appointments, so I asked her if we could use her veteran benefits. She never explicitly declined, so I had hope that it would be something that we could explore together, but after not getting anywhere after many efforts, I eventually dropped the ball and stopped fighting for that one request that should have been a demand.

She convinced herself that I was the one who turned down therapy and was to blame for our troubled marriage. At this point, I was very frustrated as I realized there was no benefit in this marriage, especially what I felt that I agreed to marry her for, her benefits. It's no secret that spouses do benefit from marrying a vet as much as the vet gets from being married. I was still using my own insurance that I was paying for while she was getting more money for the family that we created together. I was foolish. I played a game and lost terribly.

I often thought I was being the bigger person by taking the blame. I believed that I had mastered self-accountability. I prided myself on the fact that I was evolving into a mature adult. I was putting on my big girl panties, and I was putting in the hard work that it would take to keep my marriage together. So many times, I had done things, behaved badly, and received no punishment, and I suppose a part of me enjoyed the self-deprecation. Perhaps while I was convincing myself that I was making the hard choices, I chose the easy path, being complicit as the scapegoat for every misdeed. Maybe standing up for myself wasn't worth the fight anymore.

"ARE YOU FUCKING KIDDING ME?!" My sister screamed into the phone as I attempted to justify her inconceivable behavior. I pleaded with her to understand that it was my fault, that I pushed her too far. I needed her to see that I was the bad person, and she could not. The more I absorbed all the blame, the more she spat her hate and disdain for my marriage. She was relentless in her judgment. It was verbal combat the way she'd throw her words like swords on the battlefield.

She would not let me take the blame. She refused to accept that I deserved the verbal abuse inflicted upon me. Her frustration cut through the phone sharp and deadly as she let out a deep sigh, and we sat in silence. Eventually, she disconnected the call, and I felt lonely and wanted to end everything. I feared that she had given up on me. That one of my greatest warriors would not fight for me anymore. It was hard to speak with her. I was supposed to be better for her. As the big sister, it was my responsibility to be an example, and I was failing her when she needed me the most. I never wanted to create a distance between us, but I could no longer stand to see myself through her reflection on facetime.

My best friends and family grew angrier by the day. They peered through the curtains that I kept closed and saw that I hid so many things. They refused to listen to me make excuses anymore, and it felt like they were silently giving me ultimatums. If I were to build an army, it would be these people because they were ready for war. There were moments where I thought they'd come to Atlanta and force me to leave. Their love gave me comfort, and I would often feel a spark of strength, but it was extinguished by the cold body that I slept next to at night.

Note to reader

Who wins in the blame game? When we play this game, do we play for keeps? What are the rules? How do we win? What are the risks? Who invented the game, and who decides the winner? What happens to the loser? Is there a possibility of a second chance?

Blame shifting is abusive behavior and should be treated as such. The recipient of blame shifting will be left feeling resentful, confused, and often exhibit aggressive and defensive behavior. Trusting themselves and others will be difficult, as well as having low self-worth. The long-term effects of blame shifting are damaging if left unaddressed, so it is very crucial that a therapist is sought out and regular visits are maintained.

Arguing with a narcissist is pointless. The verbal game of ping pong is endless as they will most likely never admit their faults. Instead of arguing, one should aim to be calm, leveled, and assertive. Stand firm in your truth and NEVER apologize or admit to something that you did not do because once you go down that road, it will be very hard to backtrack, and the narcissist will use that to destroy your credibility. Do not pass the blame onto them out of spite; instead, hold them accountable for their behavior and focus on the facts.

Keep as much proof and evidence as you can, not only to show yourself should you feel that you may be losing grasp of reality, but it could also be useful when confronting the narcissist with facts. Focus on the problem and solution vs. who made the mistake. This will diffuse the bomb soon to come if you do not. If the narcissist proceeds with their behavior, it is time to make an exit plan and gather your support system. It will not be easy, but it is necessary, and contrary to what you believe in your moments of doubt, you can make it through. You will find peace and healing in life after dealing with a narcissist.

Chapter Seven

REACTIVE ABUSE

Reactive abuse occurs when the victim reacts to the abuse they are experiencing. The victim may scream, toss out insults, or even lash out physically at the abuser. The abuser then retaliates by telling the victim that they are, in fact, the abuser.

I wanted to share some of my personal diary entries while I was in a relationship with a narcissist. These are some of my darkest moments, and a part of my healing is to release my trauma by sharing my story. You can make it out of the dark.

ATLANTA, GA

I feel so bad. Why do I always feel like a bad person when I stand up for myself? I should know better than to respond to her, but I could not hold it in any longer. I know my people fucking LOVE me, but she keeps making me feel like my friends and family do not care about me because they did not come to visit me since we have been together. I know that's a lie, but it still messes with me. So I blew up and screamed at her. I told her she was upset that I had a family that loved me. We both ended up calling each other bitches. I mean, we were so disrespectful to each other. My anger got the best of me, so I told her if her mother was alive, she would understand the value of family and what it meant to have one. I will never forget the look on her face. I know that I hurt her. I didn't have to go that far, but I was so frustrated. She'll never let me live this down, and I hated myself for being so mean.

Today's therapy appointment was horrible, and I do not know why I even try at this point. During the session, my son told the therapist that the way I chose to correct his actions before meeting Marjorie was harsh and cruel, and Marjorie kept intervening in our session and was saying that she didn't agree with the way I disciplined my children before I met her. I explained to the therapist I was very remorseful, and when the therapist left, Marjorie and I got into a heated argument, and that's when things got out of hand. We yelled for hours. The kids started screaming. I told her that if she could do a better job as a parent, she should take care of these kids. Everyone hates me and thinks I am a bad mom. What even is a bad fucking mom??? I am over being a mom. I am over being a wife. I am over being a family. I am over life at this fucking point. Why is it that nothing ever works out for me? I work so hard to take care of my family, and they don't even see it. They don't even care, so what is the point? Why am I here?

I'm fresh out of the hospital. I am so embarrassed. Why the hell did I do that? How could I do that? So not only am I a bad mom, but I can't even commit suicide right. I downed 20 pills and two bottles of cough syrup. I knew then my life was over and the reaction of not being good enough almost cost me my life. The feeling of my heart slowing and then beating faster and then slowing again and then, black. Idk. I don't remember. I just remember being so confused, like there was just a lot going on in my head, so many voices. It was overwhelming. Marjorie contacted my family and friends in Houston, so now I have to hear their shit. They already hate this girl, and they will definitely hate her FOREVER after this. Maybe I should send the kids to Houston while I figure this shit out. I guess now that I have a clear mind, I can actually think about what I need to do or the future if I still plan on having one.

So, Marjorie just came home from an outing with Sage, and she asked me who was staying home as I was taking one of the boys out on a date. I told her that I was taking K, and she started telling me that I was supposed to take him next week. I know I told her I was taking J first, but she didn't want to listen to me. She got frustrated with me, and she started yelling about how I was a horrible mother, and she hated the way I parent MY children. I wanted to hit her so badly, like I am getting heated just thinking about it. Anyway, the tension kept building, and I felt so much rage. The next thing I know, I am charging straight to the bedroom window, and the only thing that stopped me from breaking the glass was the blinds. Now I have to pay for the stupid blinds because I let this girl get me so upset that I needed to punch, IDK, anything really. It did feel good now, but now I have to live with her calling me violent and making me feel like a shitty person.

How the hell did I end up walking on 288 and Southmore? I hate walking, and there I was walking alongside the freeway. I really just wanted to disappear from her and all of my troubles. I could have stayed in Houston with people who wouldn't make me feel worthless and stupid. I told her this trip would help my mental health, and I REALLY needed to be around family, which ended up being THE worst trip ever. It was such a disaster when we picked up the rental truck. I tried to remain calm the entire ride even though she had an attitude with me and the kids. She fought with my boys constantly. I mean, why are you arguing with kids?? She embarrassed me in front of my people like she showed her entire ass! I can't wait for this pandemic to be over so I can breathe and get away from this house.

November 9, 2020

In My Thoughts

I told Marjorie that I wanted her to die today. I was just so hurt that she called social services and the cops. This bitch is so spiteful that she is willing to do anything to hurt me and destroy me. She knows these kids are all I have, and they are what I live for. This was the ultimate betrayal. How could I forgive her after this? I swear life would be so much better without her.

Note to reader

When you put everything from this book into perspective, you will see how twisted, demented, and skilled someone with narcissistic personality disorder can be. At times it may seem like they know you better than you know yourself, and perhaps they do because they know PEOPLE. They study habits and behaviors so they can predict what will come next and act on it before you do. There will be times that your own desires and emotions aren't really yours; they are actually orchestrated by the narcissist. You are reacting exactly how they want you to, thinking exactly how they want you to think, feeling exactly how they want you to feel, which is why when you react to their abuse, it will always be in their best interest.

The narcissist thrives on pushing their victims' buttons. They want you to be filled with rage, curse, and be combative. They may even push you to the point of severe aggression but keep in mind that is their plan. This behavior gives them the ammunition that they need to label you as the abuser. You will be labeled as crazy and belligerent, and if you have a mental illness, they may suggest that you get on medication (or more medication). You will be labeled as violent and out of control, but you are none of the things that your abuser labels you as.

Breakthesilence.org compares mutual abuse and reactive abuse very clearly and concisely. Victims of reactive abuse may start to view themselves as abusive because they may react to their abuser's physical, mental, verbal, and emotional abuse. It is just that, a reaction, and BTS argues that mutual abuse is rare in situations where there is a domestic violence situation. Mutual abuse is when both parties are abusive to each other, not one party reacting to abuse or defending themselves.

So how do we break the cycle? How can we stop the inevitable? Break The Silence suggests that you think about how you will respond during the altercation with your partner. You would handle this situation similarly to how you would handle someone who is shift blaming. You should aim to remain calm but assertive. A hot temper will only make the situation worse. Again, keep as much proof as you can, they can and will have no problem calling authorities, and in so many cases, it's usually the victim who is arrested. LEAVE. Violence is never a one-time event. It will happen again. Find a safe space for you to retreat to. Your partner or loved one should never bring out the worst in you. I overindulged in her influence and underestimated myself. May we all find peace in life after dealing with a narcissist.

Chapter Eight

DISCARDING

Dis·card
/di'skärd/

Verb
get rid of (someone or something) as no longer useful or
desirable.

My heart shattered to pieces, and tears formed a lump in my throat each time I thought of life without Marjorie. Even though our marriage was extremely dysfunctional, I was acclimated to my life. I knew exactly how to respond to her angry outburst; I knew when to ignore her and when to be calm. I knew what her triggers were and how to make her content because there was no way that she could ever be happy. I knew stroking her ego would make things much easier for me and how to play the dutiful, naive, and submissive wife. It felt like I knew her so well, what my ex-wife was capable of and what she was not capable of. I learned her patterns and predicted her moods, but I would have never predicted that she would leave me.

I was aware that we were bonded through trauma. So many times, I toyed with the thought of leaving her but never could. It actually hurt to think about it. A small voice in my mind screamed faintly for me to leave, but it was overpowered by her voice which had a greater presence. Her voice told me that she loved me and that she'd always be there for me. I heard her confessions of knowing that we were so imperfect but that we were perfect for each other. She'd say that there was no one else that she'd rather spend life with but me. I was assured that our family was worth fighting for and that we were a priority to her.

Those assurances were as empty as her heart because she would disappear, but I knew that she'd come back, eventually. After an argument, she would leave for hours that seemed like a lifetime while I sat at home pacing back and forth, worrying about her but also furious. She'd even leave when we were having a good day, just disappear and come back home without any excuse for herself or where'd she'd been. I would question her about her whereabouts, but she would never give a straight or sensible answer, so I learned not to question her because she always came back home to her family, and we were her priority.

The scenarios that I would create in my mind were endless. I'd imagine that Marjorie just needed a break. She'd go to the mall, the theater, enjoy a nice lunch or dinner, indulge in a bit of self-care. Perhaps she went to her favorite park and enjoyed the Georgia air. Silence was a luxury, and she flossed in solitude. I'd like to think that she was just sitting in her truck watching Netflix. Done with her much needed time alone she would drive home realizing that she missed me, and there was even a part of me that thought that she'd return with flowers and a smile.

Another scenario that I entertained wasn't as lovely as the previous one, but it was easy to swallow. Since I was used to her dropping and picking me up whenever she felt like it, I became paranoid and obsessed with her Houdini act.

So, to keep my sanity, I would imagine that she'd storm out of the house in her moment of anger. She'd drive around angrily with a heart full of disdain as her fingers gripped the steering wheel tightly. Maybe she made the same few loops on the interstate. Maybe she went to a bar and planned her own exit plan. She pondered on our marriage and if it was truly going to last and landed at the realization that nothing ever lasts and we weren't an exception to the rule. So she drove home ready to tell me of her plans for departure, and as she looked me in the eyes, the words " I love you" would come out instead of "I'm leaving you."

I guess you can say that I had a very whimsical and fairy tale expectation of love. I would have loved to be swept off my feet. I was always one great love away from my Cinderella moment. My wife and I would live happily ever after with our kids. Heck, maybe we'd have two more for good measure. We would be everything to each other, partners, best friends, and confidants. We would take on the world, a power couple at their best. Our dreams and goals were within our grasp. Wealth would be our status and something that we could pass on to our children, but I'm ashamed to say that the only thing that we passed on to our kids during our very brief marriage was the trauma they are still dealing with to this day.

The first time Marjorie discarded me on a larger scale was in April of 2020. We were still pretty early in the Covid-19 pandemic, and I will admit that I was a bit naive about the severity of the disease. On the other hand, Marjorie was like an expert, obsessed with the news and reading articles. She introduced the idea of me quitting my job, and I obviously dismissed her silly idea. She wasn't working, and her monthly check was not enough to cover all our monthly expenses.

She explained that she could not afford to get sick, and I was at high risk since I worked in the airline industry. Unbeknownst to me, the world would give her exactly what she wanted. Soon after that conversation, the world as we knew it began to shut down along with the schools. While I was at work, Marjorie would be home with the kids, and she complained every day. It seemed like it put more of a strain on our marriage as she began to take her frustrations out on me, so I decided to take a small leave to help her with our children. That leave turned into an extended leave as the airports were closed because all flights were canceled.

We were spending too much time together, and we were NOT enjoying it at all. Even though work was mentally and emotionally draining, it still provided me with the respite that I needed from my marriage. Her mental warfare was unrelenting. Every moment was a critique. Her moods were like a tornado passing through, destroying everything in its wake. Even the kids would hide out in their room whenever they could.

I could no longer talk on the phone in my car after work, so I began to take more calls inside the house. One thing about Marjorie, she would always monitor my calls, and this day was no different. I spoke to a friend, and she hinted that she wanted me to hang up. I ignored her and resumed my conversation. I heard the keys jingle in the background, and as I turned around, she was leaving out the door. I realized that she had taken the keys to the car she purchased for me, and my heart dropped as one of my greatest fears of our marriage had just happened.

She returned hours later and informed me that she was moving out. She had booked an Airbnb for 30 days and needed to figure out whether she wanted to continue our marriage. While she was away, she continued to devalue me and our family. Marjorie admitted that she had a flawed idea that I would chase her and beg her to return home. I never begged her to come back, but I told her that ending our marriage was not an option. I attempted to rebuild what self-respect I had within those 30 days, but when she came back with false promises to do better for not only the children but our marriage, I knew that all my progress was lost, and it would be hell to get it back. She returned to her old ways, and so did my depression.

I should have told her not to stay away and use that time to search for a new place. Those 30 days should have been the end of our marriage, but I was still hopeful that our marriage would work, and I did not want to be lonely. Her return after that month showed me that she would always come back and showed her that I would always accept her no matter how long she was gone. I tricked myself into thinking that things would be different, but they couldn't be different because I was still the same person, lacking boundaries and a pushover.

The second major event was traumatic as my abandonment issues were triggered, and I did not handle it well. I planned an adventure for us to travel to Philadelphia and ride the bus to New York City. I was really looking forward to the trip because we could reconnect and create memories. We thought it would be good to rent bikes and trek our way to Times Square. While enjoying the magic of Times Square, it started to rain, and I suggested that we get a rideshare to go back to our hotel. She said that rideshares weren't running because of the protest.

After telling her that the app was still taking riders, we went back and forth for what seemed like an hour. Marjorie was always so sure of herself, and this trip was no different. In fact, her arrogance seemed magnified, so she did not take it well when I told her to give the app some time to send a driver to us. She exploded and accused me of being a know-it-all and trying to take control and plan the trip. This would be our most intense argument of the trip, and it resulted in her abandoning me in Times Square.

That foreign huge place contributed to the feelings that overwhelmed me as we stood in the midst of the protest for George Floyd. The cries for justice stirred something inside of me that I couldn't place at that time. I looked in the faces of the protestors, and I was in awe of their strength and bravery. They believed in a cause and wanted the world to know exactly how they felt. They didn't cower under the presence of the authorities. They were relentless in their convictions. It seemed we all stood there with pain in our hearts.

I booked my trip and stood in the rain for 7 minutes as my tears and the raindrops became one and rolled down my cheeks. I arrived at the hotel and awaited her return, unsure what I would say or do. Marjorie walked in dripping wet and shameless and asked me how did I get to the hotel, and I responded, "I got a rideshare," and threw in the fact that I arrived at the hotel over an hour ago. She didn't respond. She lowered her head as a somber expression flashed across her face and changed out of her soaking clothes.

That act of discard was supposed to teach me a lesson, to let me know that she was in control and had no problem leaving me. I had stepped out of place by insisting that we take the rideshare, which was not to happen again. I did ponder if insisting that we take the rideshare was even worth the discord that I created within our family and for what? Because I did not want to walk in the rain? Did I let my need to stand up for myself get in the way of enjoying our anniversary?

THE GRAND DISCARD JULY 2020

After devaluing me for months, she did what I would call The Grand Discard. It was the summer of 2020, and the kids were out for their summer break. My son's behavior became unpredictable and aggressive towards my ex-wife. He confided in me that he wanted our life to go back to when Marjorie left us the first time and expressed that he did not like where our life was and his hatred for his stepmother. He didn't like that I always seemed angry and irritated, and he felt like I was directing my frustrations towards him and his brother. My heart broke as he spoke, and I knew I had to do something different, but I did not know how.

Marjorie's behaviors and habits started changing drastically. I noticed that she would always pick fights on Wednesdays and Saturdays so she could leave the house without an explanation. I suspected that she had met someone new and questioned her about her behavior. With narcissistic charm, she told me that I was crazy and creating scenarios just to argue with her. I dropped the subject, but we would still argue about the problems in our marriage instead of working through them.

A few days after she and my eldest son had an altercation, she told me that she thought it was best that she left because our marriage was too chaotic, and the stress of our marital problems was affecting her health. She explained how she wasn't emotionally connected to me anymore and that we should live separately. I told her that if she wanted to leave, I would not fight her about it. While I didn't expect her to leave, the thought of not living under such duress anymore brought great relief to me.

Without any warning, she came home one day and said she had found a place and was moving out. I didn't say anything as she began to pack her belongings. I was shocked that she actually followed through and realized that our conversation was a heads-up and not a threat. She refused to give me her new address, and I wondered if her new dwelling was with the person that she was going to see on

Wednesdays and Saturdays. I had no idea that her move-out day would be the last day we ever shared a home again.

Note to the reader

The emotional turmoil of being repeatedly discarded is immense. You are entered into this cycle of uncertainty. It really becomes the new norm for the parties involved, so when they leave again, you will accept them again. To break this cycle, you must first be willing to let go. I wasn't ready to let go the first time my ex-wife left, and to be honest, I would have let her come back after she moved out the second time if she wanted to. I did not break the cycle, but SHE did because I was of no use to her anymore.

When you no longer provide the narcissist with the fuel they need, they will begin to discard you. The signs that they are preparing to discard you are as follows:

- They no longer create arguments. It may seem to you that they stopped caring.

- Their behavior changes drastically.

- They disappear often. Their disappearance could be for a multitude of reasons but not limited to infidelity, or they have found someone new to project their feelings upon.

- They become extremely distant

Choose yourself first. Trust your instincts and lean not into feelings of abandonment. Stick to your boundaries. You will never love the narcissist into being the person you want to be as they lack the capacity to care about anyone but themselves, so they won't care about you. They simply can't. This was my harsh reality, and it hurt realizing this as much as it did being abandoned by my ex-wife. I know that I will find commitment and security in life after dealing with a narcissist, and so will you.

Chapter Nine

THERAPY

ther·a·py
/ˈTHerəpē/

noun
treatment intended to relieve or heal a disorder.

I am no stranger to therapy. I was forced to attend therapy appointments at a very young age to deal with the trauma from the abuse from my uncle and aunt and my mother's drug addiction. It was torture for me to talk to a stranger who seemed like they were more interested in judging me than helping. I felt like my previous therapist pitied me, and I hated how that made me feel. Their probing questions brought upon an uncomfortableness that took me forever to outgrow. The thought of a stranger wanting to help me when my own family didn't made everything seem so insincere.

I attempted therapy inconsistently for 11 years, and I still could not see the value until Dekalb County forced me after my failed suicide attempt. Therapy was a requirement during my stay there, but it became less of a chore. Slowly, I opened my mind and dropped my defenses, mostly be-cause I was exhausted and needed to speak with someone about everything going on. It was therapeutic to process my emotions and unload. To speak about the things that happened to me without the fear of being judged. The probing questions didn't feel so probing, and it felt like I was in a space where I could finally start to reflect.

During my stay in the hospital, the progress that I made seemed to diminish every day once I returned home. My marriage was deteriorating, and I suffered from anxiety and depression, so as time went on, I found myself yet again going down a very dark road. It wasn't until the Grand Discard that I gathered the courage to try therapy again. My emotions were a mess, and I had no idea the direction that my life was going, but I knew I needed help. So I sought out a therapist but not just any therapist. I wanted a therapist who could understand my life as a black queer woman.

After researching, I found a database of black women therapists who specialized in lesbian relationships and military members. I felt seen, like she could be the therapist that I so desperately needed and who could possibly identify with my life experience, so I scheduled an appointment with her instantly. A week later, I had my first virtual meeting with her, and since Marjorie had moved out, I was able to express myself without being interrupted by her or her listening in on my session.

I believe the turning point during that first session was when she asked me what she could do to help get me to a different headspace. She wanted to know what I wanted to work on, so I briefed her on my marital issues and my desires to either work through them but also I knew that I really needed to leave Marjorie alone for good. I watched the therapist take notes as she listened intently, and after a few moments, she looked up at me and asked me if I was dealing with a narcissist. I responded by asking her what a narcissist was, and she began to explain in great detail, and that's when I realized that I was not crazy. I researched narcissists as soon as I arrived home. I became obsessed with learning more, and my mind became a sponge as I absorbed every detail that I could.

I continued with my therapy sessions and started to gain a strong sense of self. I learned that I am valuable, loved, and that my current life was not by happenstance. Everything I went through and will go through was already destined, so I had to take this life and mold it into a life that I cherish. I must not sacrifice my happiness. I learned how to set boundaries with everyone in my life and stand firm with those boundaries, even if it hurts. I learned that I could no longer settle for things I don't desire. Therapy provided me with the tools that I needed to learn patience. I realized that I couldn't make people love me or stay with me; they must be in my life because they want to. I began to release the pain I held onto for so many years.

My greatest discovery may have been learning my triggers: threats, false promises, loud sounds, and aggression. I become distrustful when I perceive someone as being overly nice to me, and I get enraged when I have to continually make requests of my partner or loved ones. I rarely make it past the dating phase because my instinct is to run as soon as someone makes a mistake or shows any sign of imperfection.

I wish that I could say that I am successfully managing my triggers. Every day is a new day to make progress. In times of stress, I find constructive activities to help me stay positive and full of good energy. I have found confidence by stepping outside of my comfort zone. To my surprise, I also realized that I am quite funny and provide joy to people throughout the world via social media.

I have to say, life is not perfect, but it's worth living. I realize that it is a gift. I want to be alive to see my boys grow up into handsome young men. I want to be around for my family. After dealing with a narcissist, I found a way to live my life according to my own means.

Chapter Ten

A Letter to the Narcissist

Dear Narcissists All Around The World,

Thank you for showing what a true shitty person looks like. You treated me like trash, and I only wanted to love and care for you. I wanted to make you feel whole even though you were empty and broken inside. Your heart was rotten, and your energy was vibrating on a level so low that the devil himself had to look up to you from hell, but I wanted to save you. I wanted to show you the good in people, the world, and me. I wanted you to believe in me the way that I believed in you. My goal was to build and support you.

To the narcissist I fell in love with and married, I had this dream of us taking over the world and being the best mothers we could be to our children. Our finances would grow, and so would our family. I had plans of us being indestructible and inseparable. I wanted to add value to your life, not take away from it, but you had no real intentions of loving me or giving me anything other than your inherited trauma and dysfunction. You found ways to use, abuse, mistreat, love bomb, manipulate, pass blame, gaslight, and discard someone that only saw the good in you. Someone willing to give up everything just to be there right by your side. Someone who made major sacrifices for you. Someone who only desired to be your partner, an equal, not your sidekick.

It's so unfair how you could enter my life only to ruin it, or so you thought. You must take responsibility for your own shit, drama, and toxicity. Take accountability for things you have done to people because your life will be forever full of shit until you do. You will forever lack true love and true friends. You will not prosper and grow. You will remain stuck in the same cycle living the same mediocre life.

You made me feel worthless and useless only to make your own shitty life relevant in an attempt to elevate yourself. You fucking hurt me and almost destroyed me, you narcissistic piece of shit.

I am strong. I am independent. I am worthy of true love, and I did not deserve you, and you definitely did not deserve me. The next time you think about using another human as your supply to benefit your disgraceful life, you should play these words in this letter in the back of your mind. I hope they haunt you. I hope my face and my pain haunts you. Let it be the thing that inspires you to be better, to do better.

You should know that your tricks are old. People are being

educated about you narcissistic psychopaths every day, and we are no longer taking your shit. We will no longer cower under your shadow. We are taking back our lives and living them on our own terms. We hold power, and we are healing. We are sharing our stories and spreading positivity throughout the world. We are surviving and thriving not because of you but in spite of you. I don't hate you, and I hope you find peace within your heart and life. I hope you can look at yourself in the mirror one day and truly like what you see.

Signed,

A Healed Narcissistic Abuse Survivor

Reflections

What do you love about your spouse/partner? _____

_____

_____

_____

_____

_____

_____

How does your spouse/partner treat you?

_____

_____

_____

_____

_____

_____

_____

Do you have a support team or system?

_____

_____

_____

_____

_____

_____

_____

If you were to leave your abusive partner, would you have
your own resources? If not, what is stopping you from
doing so?

_____

_____

_____

_____

_____

_____

Do you have boundaries set with your partner? Do you enforce them?

_____

_____

_____

_____

_____

_____

_____

Have you created an exit plan?

_____

_____

_____

_____

_____

_____

_____

What does your exit plan consist of?

_____

_____

_____

_____

_____

_____

_____

Can you see your life without the narcissist in your life?

_____

_____

_____

_____

_____

_____

_____

Do you believe that you are in an abusive relationship? If so, in what form of abuse does your relationship fall under?

_____

_____

_____

_____

_____

_____

_____

Do you feel safe?

_____

_____

_____

_____

_____

_____

_____

Do you know how to get assistance from your local and national resources? If not, please look at the resources provided at the back of the book.

_____

_____

_____

_____

_____

_____

_____

How do you handle stress?

_____

_____

_____

_____

_____

_____

Are you aware of your triggers, and how do you handle them?

_____

_____

_____

_____

_____

_____

_____

Are you able to look at your reflection? What do you see?

_____

_____

_____

_____

_____

_____

_____

What is the one thing you wish you could tell your future self?

_____

_____

_____

_____

_____

_____

_____

What is the one thing you wish you could tell your past self?

_____

_____

_____

_____

_____

_____

_____

Explain what love is/isn't to you?

_____

_____

_____

_____

_____

_____

_____

What is the one thing you wish you could tell your present
self?

_____

_____

_____

_____

_____

_____

_____

What is the first thing you think about when you wake up and/or last thing you think about before going to sleep?

_____

_____

_____

_____

_____

_____

_____

What are your goals?

_____

_____

_____

_____

_____

_____

_____

What are you doing to work on your goals?

_____

_____

_____

_____

_____

_____

_____

Do you feel the need to put others before yourself? If so, why?

_____

_____

_____

_____

_____

_____

_____

How do you feel when you say the word no? Why do you feel that way?

_____

_____

_____

_____

_____

_____

_____

Do I really want this person in my life? If so, why?

_____

_____

_____

_____

_____

_____

_____

Ask your partner why they are in love with you and write their answer here. For every reason they give you, ask probing questions to where you aren't given generic answers. How does their explanation make you feel?

_____

_____

_____

_____

_____

_____

_____

_____

_____

_____

_____

_____

_____

How do you think your life would be if this person were not in your life?

_____

_____

_____

_____

_____

_____

_____

Resource Page

HOW TO GET HELP

If you or someone you know is in immediate danger of domestic violence, call 911 or otherwise seek emergency help. Anyone who needs advice or support can contact the

National Domestic Violence Hotline 24/7 via:

- phone, at 800-799-7233

- live chat, at thehotline.org

- text, by texting LOVEIS to 22522

National Suicide Prevention Lifeline

- Hours: Available 24 hours.

- Languages: English, Spanish. **800-273-8255**

Crisis Text Line

Text HOME to 741741 to connect with a Crisis Counselor

Free 24/7 support at your fingertips.

About The Author

Jessica D. Washington is a flourishing entrepreneur hailing from Houston, TX. Her screwed-up past led her to seek refuge in the city of her dreams, Atlanta, GA. She found herself in rooms so big she thought they would swallow her. It turns out she was embraced by Atlanta's thriving entertainment industry. While living in The Peach State, Washington harvested a juicy career as a celebrity photographer. In a flash, her camera lens placed her on red carpets, at Grammy album release parties, stunning video shoots, and more.

At the end of this tale, she is penning a new story of resilience, confidence, and self-love. The current chapter is a page-turner highlighting her character as a motivational speaker, published author, domestic violence survivor, mental health advocate, and social media sensation. Her videos have been viewed millions of times, dubbing her as the empowering entertainer. She is showing the world that life after dealing with a narcissist can have a happy ending.

www.ingramcontent.com/pod-product-compliance
Lightning Source LLC
Chambersburg PA
CBHW050238270326
41914CB00041BA/2033/J